the TRUTH ABOUT CATS & DOGS

TOTALLY AMAZING FACTS ABOUT OUR FURRY BEST FRIENDS

by NIKKI POTTS

CAPSTONE PRESS
a capstone imprint

DOGS HAVE BEEN DOMESTICATED FOR AT LEAST 15,000 YEARS.

They are DESCENDANTS of GRAY WOLVES.

WILD CATS

DATE BACK TO PREHISTORIC TIMES.

⇦ Saber-toothed cat

DOMESTICATED CATS HAVE BEEN AROUND FOR ABOUT 8,000 YEARS.

FURRR REAL??

There are MORE than 400 DOG BREEDS.

THE UNITED STATES HAS MORE DOGS THAN ANY OTHER COUNTRY.

One legend says cats were created when a lion on **NOAH'S ARK** sneezed and **TWO KITTENS** came out!

DOGS WERE ONCE **BANNED** AS PETS IN ICELAND.

I OBJECT!

ANCIENT EGYPTIANS THOUGHT CATS WERE MAGICAL CREATURES.

The ancient Egyptian **GODDESS BASTET** had the power to **TRANSFORM** herself into a **CAT**.

THERE ARE NEARLY

90 MILLION

PET DOGS IN THE USA.

THEY ARE KEPT AS PETS IN MANY PARTS OF THE WORLD.

But in **SOME** countries, dogs are used for **FOOD!**

Say **WHAT?!**

In 1888, hundreds of thousands of MUMMIFIED CATS were discovered in an Egyptian cemetery.

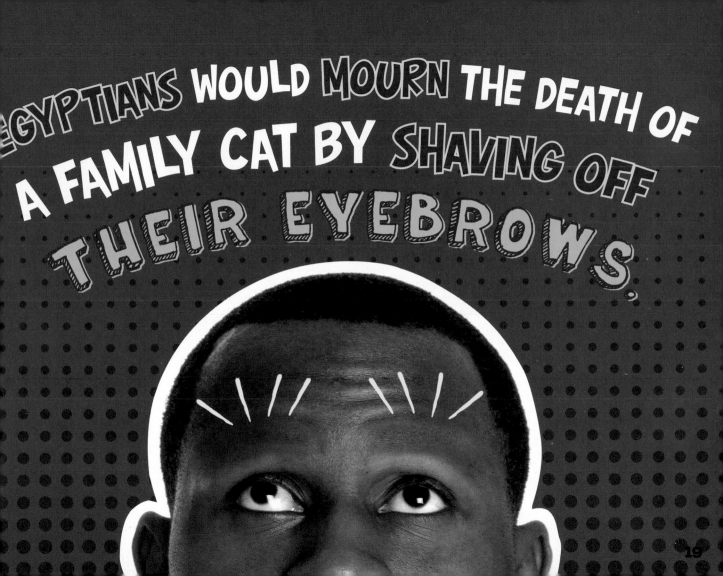

EGYPTIANS WOULD MOURN THE DEATH OF A FAMILY CAT BY SHAVING OFF THEIR EYEBROWS.

SOME WAYS PEOPLE FIRST USED DOGS WERE FOR **HUNTING** AND **PROTECTION.**

20

When livestock became DOMESTICATED, dogs HERDED and PROTECTED them as well.

The EGYPTIAN MAU is one of the OLDEST cat breeds.

THE EGYPTIAN WORD FOR CAT IS MAU.

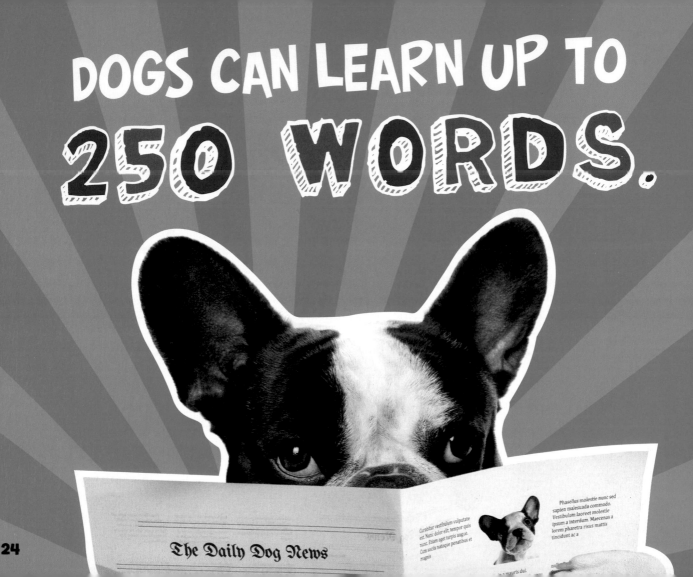

DOGS CAN LEARN UP TO 250 WORDS.

The Daily Dog News

The average dog thinks like a 2-YEAR-OLD.

THERE ARE MORE THAN **35** BREEDS OF WILD CATS.

The RUSTY-SPOTTED CAT is the SMALLEST WILD CAT.

It weighs about the same as a PINEAPPLE, at just 2.2–3.5 pounds (1–1.6 kilograms).

SOME DOGS ARE ABLE TO SMELL AND IDENTIFY CANCER IN HUMANS.

THE MAINE COON IS THE OFFICIAL CAT OF THE STATE OF MAINE.

Greetings FROM MAINE USA

A MAINE COON CAN WEIGH ALMOST **20 POUNDS** (9 KG).

That's as much as a dining chair!

MAX IS THE MOST POPULAR MALE DOG NAME.

32

BELLA IS THE MOST POPULAR FEMALE DOG NAME.

BENGALS
ARE A MIX OF

ASIAN
LEOPARD
CATS
+
DOMESTIC
CATS.

Most BENGALS love water.

DOGS HAVE A BASIC UNDERSTANDING OF MATH.

BORDER COLLIES ARE ONE OF THE SMARTEST DOG BREEDS.

Just call me **EINSTEIN!**

THE WORLD'S LONGEST

DOMESTIC CAT WAS A MAINE COON NAMED

MYMAINS STEWART GILLIGAN.

HE WAS 48.5 INCHES (123 CENTIMETERS) LONG.

THE GERMAN SHEPHERD IS THE TOP POLICE AND MILITARY DOG BREED.

OFFICER WOOF, reporting for duty.

The movie *Megan Leavey* is based on a TRUE STORY about a U.S. MARINE and her COMBAT DOG, SERGEANT REX.

A DOMESTIC CAT set a RECORD SPEED of

30 MILES

(48.3 KILOMETERS)

PER HOUR.

THAT'S **FASTER** THAN USAIN BOLT!

WHAAAT?

A DOG HAS 200-300 MILLION SCENT RECEPTORS IN ITS NOSE.

The **OLDEST** cat lived to be **38 YEARS** AND 3 DAYS OLD.

46

That's about **170** in human years!

A DOG CAN SMELL AT LEAST **1,000 TIMES** BETTER THAN A HUMAN.

Like HUMANS, DOGS can have seasonal ALLERGIES.

ACHOO!

A U.K. millionaire left **12.5 MILLION DOLLARS** to his cat, **BLACKIE,** after he died.

A dog's brain releases the "happy chemical," **OXYTOCIN,** when spending time with some humans and other dogs.

Life is pretty **AWESOME** right now!

DOGS CAN ALSO FEEL JEALOUS!

ACCORDING TO GUINNESS WORLD RECORDS, THE MOST EXPENSIVE CAT WAS PURCHASED FOR $24,000.

DOGS HAVE AROUND 1,700 TASTE BUDS.

HUMANS HAVE ABOUT 9,000!

CATS can make more than 100 SOUNDS.

Most ADULT CATS only **MEOW** to communicate with HUMANS.

THE **WETNESS** OF A DOG'S NOSE IS ACTUALLY A **THIN LAYER** OF MUCUS.

THE WETNESS HELPS THE DOG **SMELL.**

A CAT CAN RECOGNIZE ITS OWNER'S VOICE.

BUT it often chooses to IGNORE it!

63

A DOG'S NORMAL BODY TEMPERATURE IS 101–102.5 DEGREES FAHRENHEIT (38.3–39.2 DEGREES CELSIUS).

A small dog's heart BEATS between 100–140 TIMES PER MINUTE.

A CAT'S EAR IS CONTROLLED BY

33

DIFFERENT MUSCLES.

Cats can move their ears **180 DEGREES,** and separately.

OVER 40% OF DOGS SLEEP IN BED WITH THEIR OWNERS.

ALMOST 70% of dog owners think their **DOG KNOWS** when a **STORM** is coming.

CATS CAN HEAR SOUNDS UP TO ABOUT 64 kHz.

HUMANS can only HEAR up to about 20 kHz.

A SPECIAL MEMBRANE IN A DOG'S EYES HELPS IT SEE AT NIGHT.

THE MEMBRANE IS CALLED THE TAPETUM LUCIDUM.

ALL CATS CAN RETRACT THEIR CLAWS

except for the cheetah!

CHEETAHS are the FASTEST mammals.

THEY CAN RUN MORE THAN 62 MILES (100 km) PER HOUR.

DO YOUR DOG'S PAWS SMELL LIKE CORN CHIPS OR POPCORN?

This BACTERIA growing on your DOG'S PAWS is called "FRITO FEET."

All cats have NATURAL HUNTING instincts.

CATS HAVE PLAYED A PART IN THE

EXTINCTION

OF 33 DIFFERENT ANIMAL SPECIES.

PUPPIES CAN SLEEP AS MUCH AS
20 HOURS A DAY!

They are also born DEAF and BLIND.

Cats' claws all POINT BACK toward their limbs.

Because of the CURL in its claws, A CAT CAN'T CLIMB down a tree HEADFIRST!

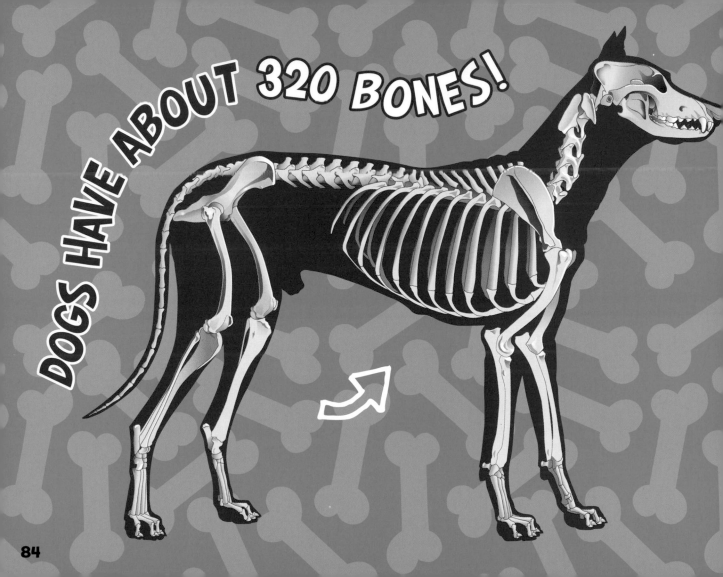

DOGS HAVE ABOUT 320 BONES!

84

PUPPIES have 28 TEETH.

ADULT dogs have 42 TEETH.

CATS can SURVIVE FALLS from HIGH AREAS.

Their bodies automatically TWIST AROUND to land on their FEET.

CATS CAN SQUEEZE INTO SMALL SPACES

BECAUSE THEY HAVE FREE-FLOATING CLAVICLES.

IT IS A NATURAL INSTINCT FOR DOGS TO SPIN BEFORE LYING DOWN. DOGS NATURALLY CURL UP WHEN THEY SLEEP.

ZZ ZZZZ

This position **PROTECTS** vital organs and keeps dogs **WARM**.

MOST CATS DON'T LIKE BEING IN WATER.

WET FUR can be HEAVY and COLD

A dog can SENSE a person's ANXIETY.

PETTING A DOG CAN LOWER YOUR BLOOD PRESSURE.

Cats move their **RIGHT** feet first and then their **LEFT**.

MOCHI THE ST. BERNARD HOLDS THE WORLD RECORD FOR LONGEST DOG TONGUE AT 7.31 INCHES (18.58 CM) LONG.

A CAT NAMED JAKE HOLDS THE WORLD RECORD FOR THE MOST TOES.

HE HAS 28!

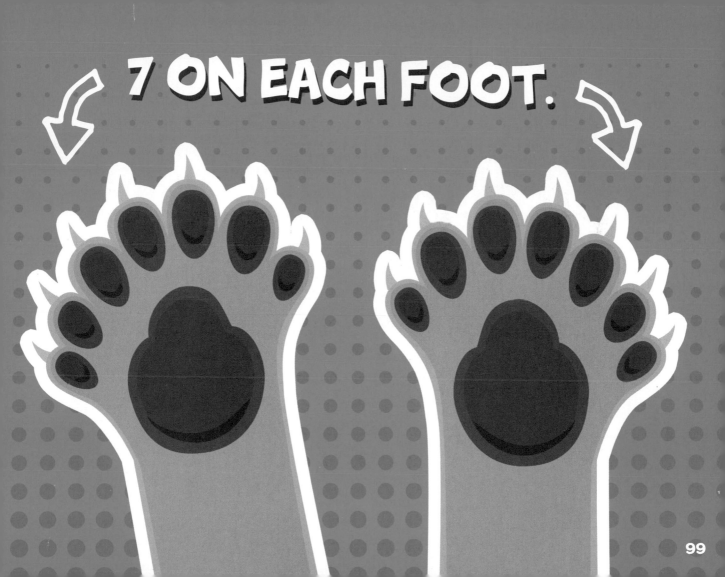

An **AUSTRALIAN CATTLE DOG** named **BLUEY** lived to **29 YEARS** and **5 MONTHS** old.

CONGRATULATIONS

He holds the world record for **OLDEST DOG.**

THE FAMOUS AUTHOR ERNEST HEMINGWAY HAD A POLYDACTYL CAT.

That's a cat with EXTRA toes!

BASENJIS HAVE BEEN HANGING OUT WITH HUMANS FOR A LONG TIME!

IN FACT, SOME PEOPLE SAY BASENJIS WERE GIVEN TO EGYPTIAN PHARAOHS AS GIFTS.

Do your cat's **WHISKERS** and **PAWS** twitch while it's sleeping? If so, it's most likely **DREAMING!**

A GROWTH HORMONE IS RELEASED WHEN A KITTEN IS SLEEPING.

WOOO! AWWOOO!

BASENJIS DON'T BARK—THEY YODEL!

CATS SLEEP FOR ABOUT 70% OF THEIR LIVES.

That's 16 hours per day of beauty rest!

UP TO 50%

OF A CAT'S WAKING HOURS ARE SPENT

CLEANING ITSELF.

The
WORLD'S
SHORTEST
dog is a
CHIHUAHUA
named
MILLY.

At just **3.8 INCHES** (9.7 CM) **TALL,** she's shorter than a **CAN OF SODA!**

UNLIKE HUMANS, CATS CAN DRINK SOME SALT WATER.

THEIR KIDNEYS FILTER OUT THE SALT.

NORWEGIAN LUNDEHUNDS HAVE **SIX TOES** ON EACH FOOT.

They can **CLOSE THEIR EARS** and **TIP THEIR HEADS**

ALL THE WAY BACK.

YOU ACTUALLY SHOULDN'T GIVE YOUR CAT MILK!

MOST ARE LACTOSE INTOLERANT!

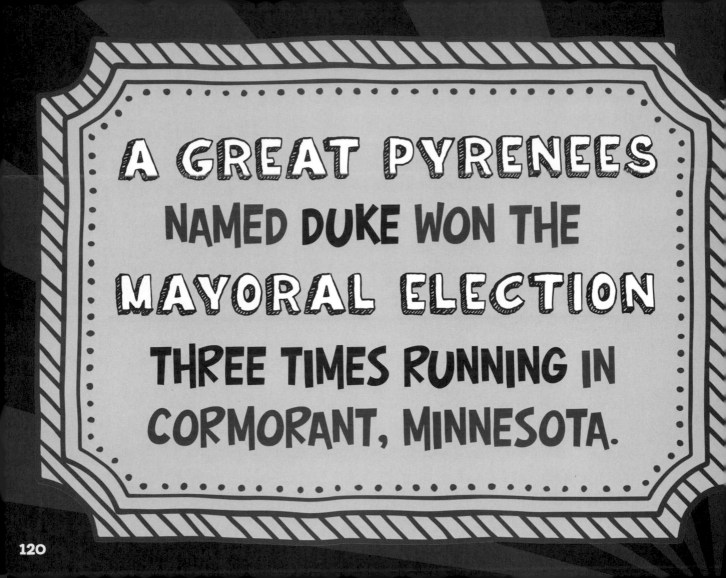

A GREAT PYRENEES NAMED DUKE WON THE MAYORAL ELECTION THREE TIMES RUNNING IN CORMORANT, MINNESOTA.

CATS HAVE **AN EXTRA** ORGAN THAT LETS THEM **"TASTE"** THE AIR.

It is called the Jacobson's organ.

CATS CANNOT TASTE SWEETS.

NEWFOUNDLANDS

HAVE WEBBED FEET!

They are also known as "Newfies."

THE BUMPS
ON A CAT'S NOSE ARE
UNIQUE
TO EACH CAT.

They are like a human's fingerprints.

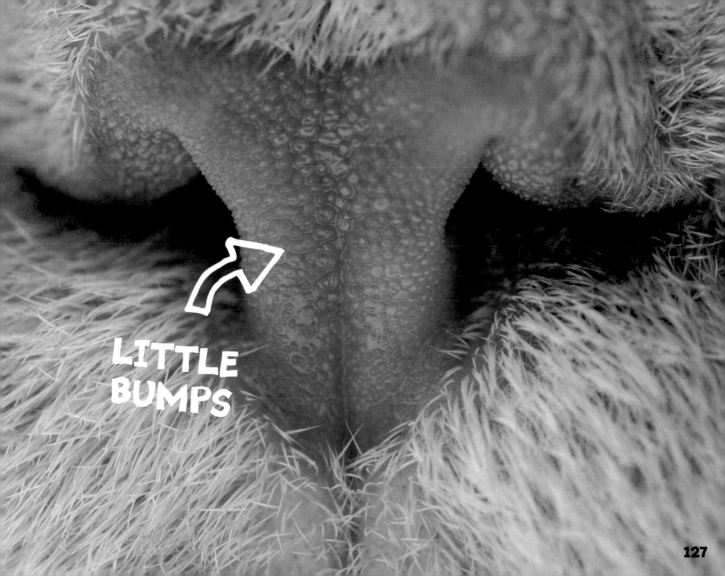

LITTLE BUMPS

Dalmatian puppies are born all WHITE!

They develop their SPOTS later on in life.

130

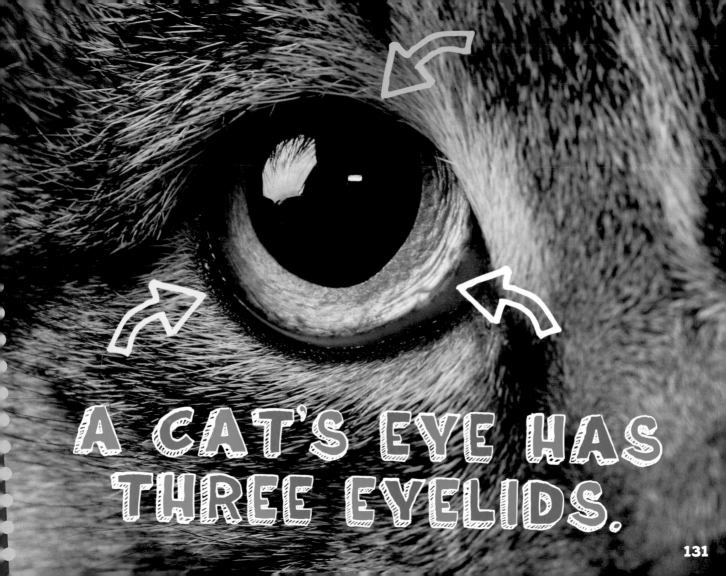

A CAT'S EYE HAS THREE EYELIDS.

A BORDER COLLIE NAMED CHASER IS THOUGHT TO BE THE WORLD'S SMARTEST DOG.

SHE RECOGNIZES THE NAMES OF MORE THAN 1,000 OBJECTS!

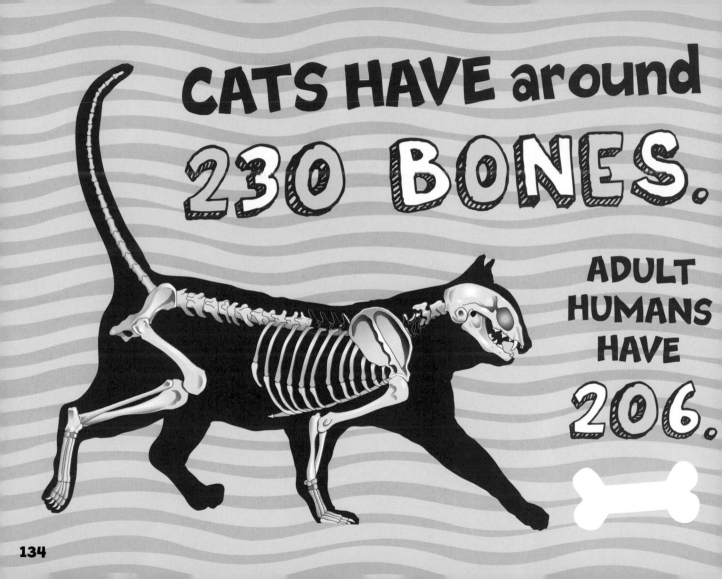

CATS HAVE around 230 BONES.

ADULT HUMANS HAVE 206.

ADULT CATS HAVE 30 TEETH.

ORIENT, A GERMAN SHEPHERD GUIDE DOG, successfully led his BLIND OWNER through the APPALACHIAN TRAIL.

The trek took 8 MONTHS.

WHISKERS help cats determine if they can FIT INTO A SPACE.

A CAT'S WHISKERS TYPICALLY GROW TO BE AS LONG AS THE CAT IS WIDE.

FAT CAT = LONG WHISKERS!

DOGS CAN BE TRAINED TO HELP PEOPLE WHO ARE HAVING SEIZURES.

They lie next to their owners to PREVENT INJURY.

MOST CATS HAVE STRIPES, SPOTS, OR ROSETTES.

ALBINO CATS are **RARE.** They are born without **PIGMENTATION,** or **COLOR.**

Dogs have at least 18 MUSCLES in each ear.

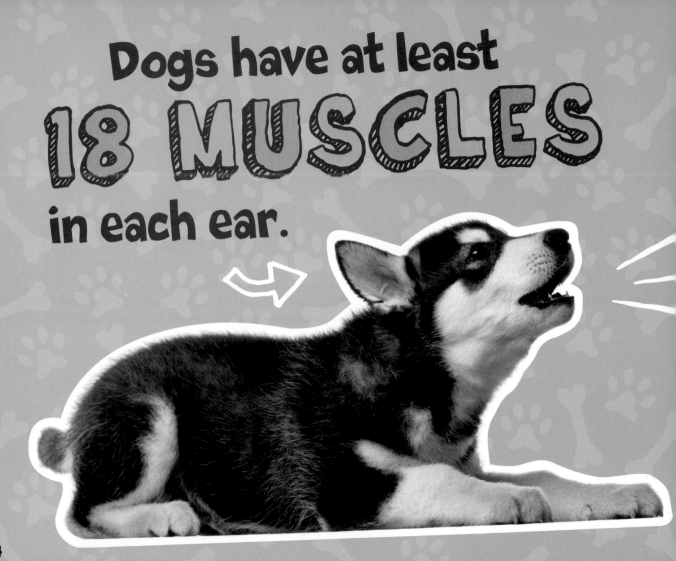

THEY CAN SHUT OFF THEIR INNER EAR TO DROWN OUT DISTRACTING SOUNDS.

A GROUP of CATS is called a "CLOWDER".

What are you LOOKIN' AT?

FEMALE feral cats often stay in small groups.

MALES are typically alone.

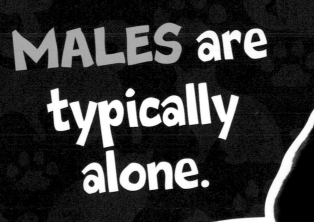

BASSET HOUNDS

have some of the **LONGEST EARS** of any breed.

If I flap them hard enough, do you think **I COULD FLY?!**

SOME MEASURE
10 INCHES
(25.4 CM)
LONG!

CATS HAVE SWEAT GLANDS IN THEIR PAWS.

These GLANDS also give off a SCENT that cats use to mark their TERRITORY.

A SERVICE DOG NAMED KIRSCH RECEIVED AN HONORARY DEGREE FROM JOHNS HOPKINS UNIVERSITY.

(HE ATTENDED EVERY CLASS WITH HIS OWNER, CARLOS.)

MOST FEMALE CATS ARE RIGHT-PAWED.

MOST MALE CATS ARE LEFT-PAWED.

155

DOGS CAN HEAR SOUNDS OF 35,000 VIBRATIONS PER SECOND.

HUMANS CAN ONLY HEAR **20,000** VIBRATIONS PER SECOND.

A **FEMALE CAT** is called a **QUEEN** or a **MOLLY**.

A **MALE CAT** is called a **TOM**.

"KITTY"

IS ONE OF THE TOP CAT NAMES.

KITTY

It's said that the BRUSSELS GRIFFON breed was the inspiration for EWOK characters in the STAR WARS movies.

May the **PAWS** be with you!

A LITTER is a group of kittens born at the same time.

LITTER is also what domestic cats **PEE** and **POOP** in.

POMERANIANS

WEIGH JUST 7-10 POUNDS

(3.2-4.5 KG).

That's about the same weight as the average watermelon.

BUT THEY ARE TOUGH POOCHES! THEY'RE KNOWN FOR BARKING AT MUCH LARGER DOGS.

AN AILUROPHILE IS A CAT LOVER.

A CHIWEENIE

is a cross between a CHIHUAHUA and a DACHSHUND.

+

ALTHOUGH SMALL, CHIWEENIES **BARK** TO PROTECT LOVED ONES. THEY CAN BE GREAT WATCHDOGS!

SOME SAY SIR ISAAC NEWTON INVENTED

THE CAT DOOR.

It is believed he may have cut a door for a MAMA CAT and, of course, a smaller door for HER KITTENS.

MANNY THE FRENCHIE IS A FAMOUS FRENCH BULLDOG.

He gained popularity on INSTAGRAM, where his owner POSTED pictures of him SNOOZING IN A SINK.

HE WAS NAMED ONE OF THE MOST INFLUENTIAL PETS IN 2017.

Z Z Z Z Z Z Z

PRESIDENT LINCOLN WAS A CAT LOVER AND OFTEN BROUGHT HOME STRAYS.

TABBY and DIXIE, two of Lincoln's cats, often ate FROM THE DINNER TABLE!

DOGS HAVE SOME SWEAT GLANDS IN THEIR PAWS.

But
PANTING
is their
main way of
COOLING
OFF.

Owning a CAT LOWERS a person's RISK of having a STROKE or HEART ATTACK.

IT IS A MYTH THAT DOGS ONLY SEE IN BLACK AND WHITE.

DOG VISION

THEY SEE SOME COLOR, BUT NOT AS VIVIDLY AS HUMANS.

HUMAN VISION

IN THE UNITED STATES, SOME CONSIDER BLACK CATS BAD LUCK.

IN AUSTRALIA, BLACK CATS ARE THOUGHT TO BRING GOOD LUCK.

MOST DOGS HAVE **PINK** TONGUES.

BUT CHOW CHOWS AND SHAR-PEIS HAVE BLACK TONGUES!

Disneyland has more than 200 CATS.

THE CATS HUNT MICE IN THE PARK AT NIGHT.

GREYHOUNDS ARE THE FASTEST DOG BREED.

THEY CAN RUN UP TO **45 MILES** (72.4 KM) **PER HOUR!**

CAT ISLAND

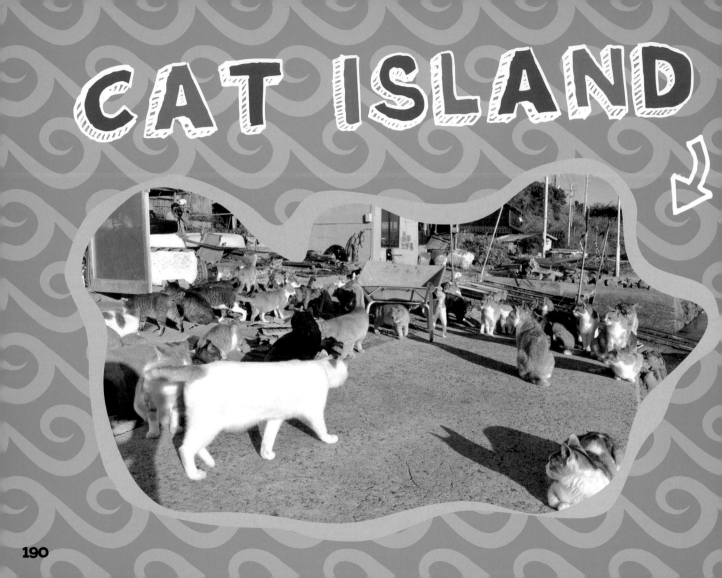

HUNDREDS OF CATS LIVE ON AN ISLAND IN JAPAN.

The human residents have created a cat shrine in the middle of the island.

Most dog owners give their pets GIFTS on BIRTHDAYS and SPECIAL OCCASIONS.

MOST ALSO INCLUDE THEIR PUP ON THE FAMILY HOLIDAY CARD.

CIVET CATS in Southeast Asia and Africa EAT

COFFEE BERRIES.

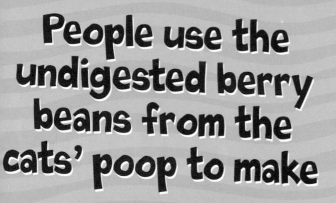

CAT POOP

People use the undigested berry beans from the cats' poop to make

COFFEE.

195

SERVICE DOGS PEE AND POOP ON COMMAND!

196

One study says that some dogs align themselves with EARTH'S MAGNETIC FIELD while they POOP.

STUBBS THE CAT

was **MAYOR** of Talkeetna, Alaska, for **20 YEARS**.

His office was located at Nagley's Store.

GEORGE WASHINGTON LOVED DOGS.

He had a **FRENCH HOUND** named **VULCAN** and a **DALMATIAN** named **MADAM MOOSE.**

THE AZTECS ONCE WORSHIPED A HAIRLESS DOG BREED CALLED

XOLOITZCUINTLI.

(show-lo-eets-kweent-lee)

THE DOGS WERE THOUGHT TO PROTECT HOMES FROM EVIL SPIRITS.

A CAT NAMED SOPHIE SMITH HAS THE LONGEST FUR OF ANY CAT.

Her fur is
10.11 INCHES
(25.68 cm)
LONG!

Are you a fan of FANG from the *HARRY POTTER* movies?

In real life, full-grown **NEAPOLITAN MASTIFFS** can weigh over

150 POUNDS

(68 KG)!

☆ LIL BUB ☆

IS A PERMA-KITTEN.

She will have **KITTEN FEATURES** for her **ENTIRE LIFE**. Her lower jaw is shorter than her top jaw, and her teeth also never grew in.

It is a MYTH that dogs feel GUILT.

YOUR DOG IS LIKELY FEELING **FEAR** INSTEAD.

FELICETTE

OR "ASTROCAT"
WAS THE
FIRST CAT
IN **OUTER**
SPACE.

She was in space for **15 MINUTES** before returning to Earth.

INDEX